The Search for

Ellen Catala

Contents

Rigby

A Harcourt Achieve Imprint

www.Rigby.com
1-800-531-5015

CHAPTER ONE

Why Did Europeans Begin Exploring?

Today we know that the earth is round and has seven continents. We no longer fear sailing off the edge of the earth or into a steaming hot sea filled with sea monsters. But hundreds of years ago in Europe, things were different.

People knew very little about the shape and size of the earth then. Most people believed that the earth was flat. They also believed frightening stories about monstrous animals and scary people who lived in other parts of the world.

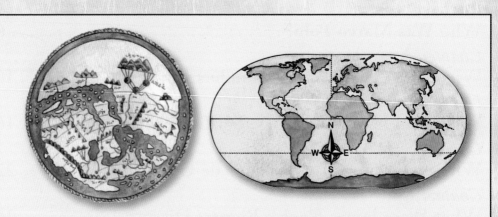

People have discovered a lot about the world in their searches for new lands. A mapmaker from Morocco painted the world map on the left in 1154. South is at the top of this map! A modern world map is on the right.

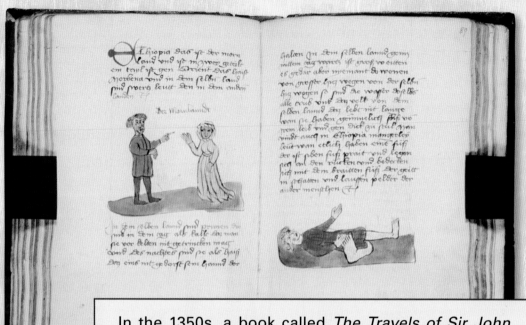

In the 1350s, a book called *The Travels of Sir John Mandeville* included strange descriptions of faraway people and places. Many people who read this book believed it was true.

Europeans were curious, and they thought being able to travel to these new places would change the way everyone thought of the world. As it turned out, their travels actually changed the world itself.

Explorers would bring many wonderful things to the new places they discovered, such as new animals, new foods, and better medicine. But they also brought many bad things, such as new diseases and even slavery. Their arrival meant that nothing would ever again be the same.

Europeans most wanted to reach the Indies, the name they gave to lands now known as India, China, Japan, and surrounding areas. They wanted to reach a group of islands near the equator called the Spice Islands. The people there knew how to make silk and grow spices. Europeans wanted silk for their clothing, but mostly they wanted spices. At that time, a spoonful of spice such as pepper, nutmeg, or cloves was worth as much as gold!

Silk is made from the cocoons of silkworm moths. In the past, only the Chinese knew how to raise silkworm moths and make silk cloth from their cocoons.

Europeans wanted to open new **trade routes** to the Indies so they would be able to get more silk, spices, and other goods. They also thought they might find gold and jewels there.

Before refrigerators were invented, it was hard to keep meat fresh, so people sometimes ate meat that was a little spoiled. They used spices to cover up the bad taste.

Who Was Marco Polo?

Marco Polo was a great explorer. Born in 1254, he lived in Venice, Italy, where a lot of trade happened. Marco grew up seeing ships arrive that were filled with silks, spices, and other goods. He knew these things were important to the people of Europe.

This is an artist's portrait of Marco Polo. By the time Marco was 20, he knew several East Asian languages as a result of his travels.

When Marco was 15 years old, his father and uncle returned from China. They had been gone since before Marco was born, and he never thought he would meet them. They told amazing stories about their adventures, including their time spent with Kublai Khan, the ruler of China.

This art shows Kublai Khan handing Nicolo Polo, Marco Polo's father, a golden tablet. The tablet was a kind of passport that Nicolo could show as he passed through the land, so no one would harm him.

When Marco's father and uncle traveled back to China in 1271, they took Marco with them. They traveled from Venice through much of Europe and Asia. Along the way, they met many people of different cultures and religions.

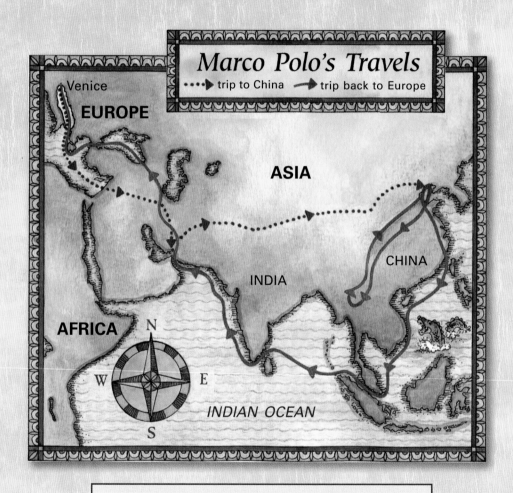

Marco Polo's Travels
••••▶ trip to China   ➡ trip back to Europe

Venice
EUROPE
ASIA
CHINA
INDIA
AFRICA
N
W   E
S
INDIAN OCEAN

This map shows the path followed by Marco Polo on his journey to China.

They arrived at Kublai Khan's summer palace three years later with many stories to tell. Marco was a good storyteller, and Kublai Khan was charmed. He sent Marco into many parts of China as his representative.

Marco, his father, and his uncle returned to Venice 20 years later. They brought back riches, but no one believed their stories. Marco lived to be 70 years old, and he wrote a book about everything he had seen.

Marco Polo returned to Europe with useful information about many Chinese inventions. The Chinese invented the magnetic compass—an important tool used by later explorers. Instead of having a needle like today's compasses, the Chinese compass used a pointer that looked like a spoon.

CHAPTER THREE

What Did Christopher Columbus Find?

One person who owned a copy of Marco Polo's book was Christopher Columbus. Born in 1451 in Genoa, Italy, Columbus was the son of a weaver, but he grew up dreaming of traveling the seas. Like Marco Polo, he watched with excitement as ships arrived at **port**, filled with goods from other parts of the world.

Christopher Columbus

This edition of Marco Polo's book was owned by Christopher Columbus. Columbus wrote the notes that can be seen off to the sides.

10

Columbus became an experienced sea captain and moved to Portugal, where people talked about finding new sea routes to the Indies. Columbus felt the best route would be across what was known as the Ocean Sea (Atlantic Ocean). No European had ever sailed across it. Columbus thought it was much smaller than it was and that China, Japan, and India were just on the other side.

Before Christopher Columbus sailed across the Atlantic Ocean, some people called it the Sea of Darkness. They thought it was filled with sea monsters.

Years passed before Columbus could convince a royal leader to give him money for the journey. Finally King Ferdinand and Queen Isabella of Spain agreed. In 1492 Columbus left with 90 men and 3 ships, the Santa María, the Niña, and the Pinta. The trip was difficult, but Columbus wanted to reach the Indies and win the respect of the whole world. He also hoped the trip would make him rich.

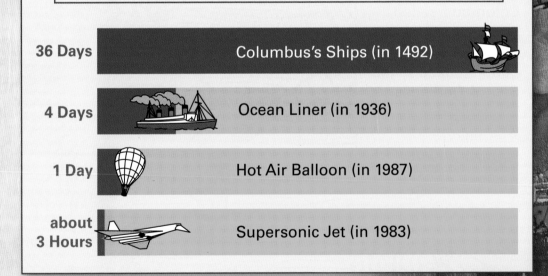

Time it Takes to Cross the Atlantic Ocean

36 Days	Columbus's Ships (in 1492)
4 Days	Ocean Liner (in 1936)
1 Day	Hot Air Balloon (in 1987)
about 3 Hours	Supersonic Jet (in 1983)

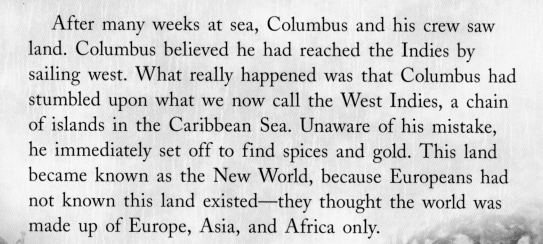

After many weeks at sea, Columbus and his crew saw land. Columbus believed he had reached the Indies by sailing west. What really happened was that Columbus had stumbled upon what we now call the West Indies, a chain of islands in the Caribbean Sea. Unaware of his mistake, he immediately set off to find spices and gold. This land became known as the New World, because Europeans had not known this land existed—they thought the world was made up of Europe, Asia, and Africa only.

Columbus and his crew first landed in the northern part of the West Indies, known as the Bahamas. Because he thought he was in the Indies, he called the people he met there Indians.

Columbus made several trips between Europe and these new lands. He founded European settlements there and explored many islands, including San Salvador, Cuba, Jamaica, Puerto Rico, and Haiti. He also explored some of the coast of Central and South America.

Certain foods, such as pineapples and potatoes, were unknown in Europe until Columbus brought them back on his ships. Here, Columbus is shown trading with native people.

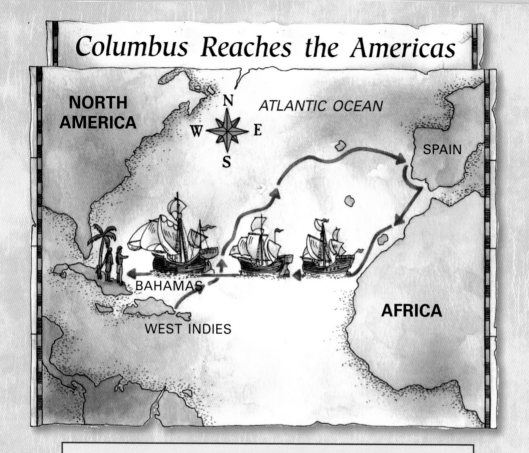

Columbus Reaches the Americas

NORTH AMERICA

ATLANTIC OCEAN

SPAIN

BAHAMAS

WEST INDIES

AFRICA

This map shows the route taken by Columbus on his first voyage across the Atlantic.

He had found the West Indies, but Columbus returned to Spain disappointed. He had not found the gold, jewels, and spices he had been searching for. He died in 1506 still thinking he had found a trade route from Europe to Asia. He had not reached Asia, but he had opened the door for future explorers and for the European **settlement** of North and South America.

CHAPTER FOUR

What Did Ferdinand Magellan Discover?

Ferdinand Magellan was born in Portugal in 1480. As members of a noble family, he and his brothers worked as assistants in the Portuguese royal court. At the court Magellan heard stories of Christopher Columbus, who had been there to see King John of Portugal. Magellan also learned about **navigation** and the search for trade routes to the Spice Islands.

FERDINAND MAGELLANUS.

Ferdinand Magellan

Magellan longed to go to sea. He, too, thought he could become rich by finding gold and spices. When the royal court decided to send ships to claim parts of the Indies for Portugal, Magellan went as a sailor and a soldier.

Explorers such as Columbus and Magellan used hourglasses like this one to tell time and to navigate.

Once he had experience as a sailor, Magellan wanted to sail directly to the Spice Islands and claim them for Portugal. The king of Portugal said no, so Magellan asked the king of Spain. After studying maps of the journeys Columbus took, Magellan believed there was a water passage through the Americas that led to the Indies.

The king of Spain agreed to give him ships, and Magellan set sail in 1519. Magellan and his crew first sailed to South America. They explored the coast as they searched for a passageway to the ocean on the other side.

Magellan set sail with 5 ships. Only the Victoria, shown here, made it through the entire voyage.

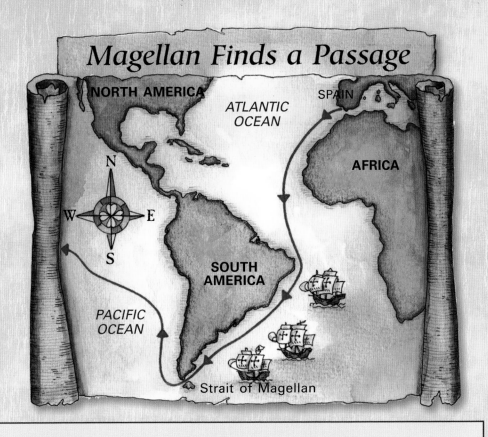

Magellan Finds a Passage

NORTH AMERICA

ATLANTIC OCEAN

SPAIN

AFRICA

N

W   E

S

SOUTH AMERICA

PACIFIC OCEAN

Strait of Magellan

Magellan's crew knew they had found a passageway from one ocean to the other when the water remained salty. Magellan called this passageway The Strait of All Saints. It was later renamed the Strait of Magellan.

One day in 1520, the ships were caught in a storm. The sailors were afraid they would crash into the coast. At the last minute they saw a small opening in the coastline and steered the ships into it. It was the passage they had been looking for!

Magellan and his crew did not know how difficult the journey would be over the Great South Sea. Magellan renamed this sea the Pacific Ocean because it was so peaceful. But its peacefulness proved to be a problem. Without wind in their sails, the ships bobbed and floated under the blazing sun for 98 days. Many sailors starved to death waiting to find land again.

When the **expedition** reached the Spice Islands, Magellan was no longer a part of it. He had died on April 27, 1521, in the nearby Philippine Islands. One of his ships finally returned to Spain, where the sailors were greeted as heroes for being the first people ever to have sailed all the way around the world.

This picture shows all 5 ships in Magellan's fleet sailing in the Pacific Ocean.

First Around the World

This map shows the route Magellan's ships took around the world.

Chapter Five

Where Did Francisco Vasquez de Coronado Travel?

Francisco Vasquez de Coronado was born in Spain in 1510, and by that time, European settlements now dotted the New World. When King Ferdinand sent Antonio de Mendoza to New Spain (Mexico), Mendoza brought his friend Coronado with him.

Francisco Vasquez de Coronado

A U.S. postage stamp from 1940 shows Coronado setting out on his journey. He is wearing a golden suit of armor and is riding a white horse. His army can be seen behind him.

Coronado became a respected governor in New Spain, but he wanted to find the famous cities of gold that many people believed existed somewhere in the New World. He wanted to claim these cities for Spain and earn wealth and glory for his home country. Like Marco Polo, his explorations would take him through deserts and over land that was very difficult to cross. Unlike Marco Polo, who traveled with a few men, Coronado traveled with an army of soldiers and many servants.

From 1540–1542 Coronado and his army went to many places, fighting the **native people** and doing whatever they could to stay alive. They traveled into what is now the southwestern and midwestern parts of the United States. They saw the Mississippi River, the Grand Canyon, and the Great Plains. Coronado wasn't impressed with these sights because he was only interested in finding gold.

Coronado's Travels

Coronado and his army traveled north, up the western coast of New Spain (Mexico) into Tierra Nueva (the United States) and back.

Coronado traveled hundreds of miles and searched for two years, but he never found any gold. Tired and disappointed, he and the surviving members of his group returned to New Spain. Coronado died in Mexico City in 1554. His exploration was important because it laid the groundwork for later Spanish settlement of Mexico and the southwestern United States.

Coronado claimed Quivira (part of Kansas) and many other parts of the United States for Spain. He had followed a guide there, who told him stories about a king who rode in a golden boat and people who ate from silver and gold dishes.

CHAPTER SIX

What Were James Cook's Biggest Discoveries?

James Cook was another boy who dreamed of traveling the seas. He was born to an English farming family in 1728 and later joined the British Navy. At the time, Great Britain was at war with France. Cook's first mission in the Navy was to bring British soldiers to Canada.

James Cook was a caring leader and an excellent mapmaker. Many members of his crew went on to become leaders of their own expeditions after their travels with him.

Cook was expert at using navigational instruments such as these.

Cook was very good at reading maps, making charts, and studying shorelines. He was also interested in astronomy, and he could navigate using the sun, stars, and special instruments. On one journey of exploration, Cook observed an eclipse of the sun. An eclipse happens when the sun's light is blocked by the moon. He wrote a paper about it and sent it to the Royal Society of London.

Later, when the Society was looking for someone to lead an expedition to Tahiti to observe another eclipse, they asked Cook. He was delighted and took the task very seriously. By 1768 his ship was packed with the necessary supplies, including onions and pickled cabbage to provide Vitamin C for his crew. Cook believed that Vitamin C prevented **scurvy**, a serious disease that sickened sailors at sea.

Cook's ship, the Endeavor, was solidly built and filled with food, warm clothing, medicines, science equipment, and small gifts for trading with the Pacific Islanders.

The British Navy asked Cook to continue this journey. They thought a huge continent might be in the Southern **Hemisphere**, balancing the continents in the Northern Hemisphere. They wanted Cook to look for it. Cook never found this continent, but he did find a smaller one—Australia—as well as New Zealand and other islands in the South Pacific.

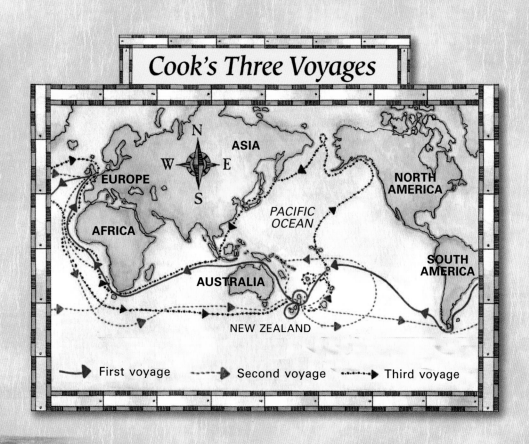

Cook's Three Voyages

First voyage ••• Second voyage ••• Third voyage

On his second voyage, Cook tried to reach the South Pole. However his ships could not sail through the heavy ice. On his third voyage, he discovered the Hawaiian Islands, where the native people thought he was a god.

Cook then explored the coasts of western Canada and Alaska, recording every detail of the coastlines. He returned to Hawaii in 1779, but wasn't greeted with friendliness this time. The chiefs disliked his power over their people. A fight broke out, and Cook was killed.

The Explorers and Their Journeys

1271
Marco Polo begins his travels to China.

1200

1400

1492
Columbus reaches the Americas.

By the time James Cook died in 1779, a lot had changed in Europe and the world. Most people now knew the world was round and the number, size, and shape of the seas and the continents (except Antarctica). What had started out as a simple quest for glory and riches became known as the "Age of Exploration."

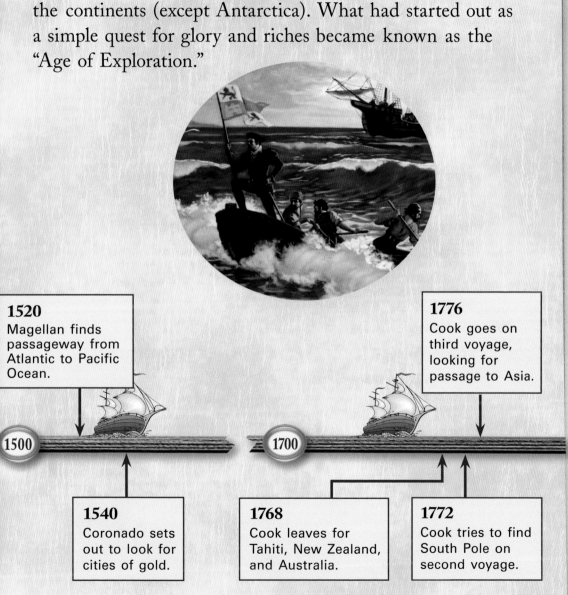

1520
Magellan finds passageway from Atlantic to Pacific Ocean.

1776
Cook goes on third voyage, looking for passage to Asia.

1500

1700

1540
Coronado sets out to look for cities of gold.

1768
Cook leaves for Tahiti, New Zealand, and Australia.

1772
Cook tries to find South Pole on second voyage.

Glossary

expedition people and supplies going on a trip to explore

hemisphere one half of Earth, as it is divided by the equator or by the Prime Meridian – an imaginary line that runs north and south

native people first people to live in a region or area

navigation science of steering a ship along a chosen course

port place from which ships come and go

settlement group of people living together in a new place for the first time

scurvy disease that affects sailors caused by a lack of Vitamin C in their diet

trade routes paths on land or sea that connect buyers and sellers of goods

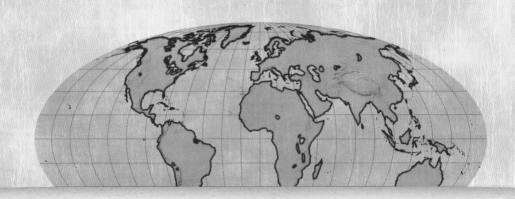